Henry George Bonavia Hunt

The glories of the man of sorrows

Sermons preached during Lent at the parish church of St. James's Piccadilly

Henry George Bonavia Hunt

The glories of the man of sorrows
Sermons preached during Lent at the parish church of St. James's Piccadilly

ISBN/EAN: 9783741164880

Manufactured in Europe, USA, Canada, Australia, Japa

Cover: Foto ©Lupo / pixelio.de

Manufactured and distributed by brebook publishing software (www.brebook.com)

Henry George Bonavia Hunt

The glories of the man of sorrows

THE GLORIES OF THE MAN OF SORROWS.

The Glories
of
The Man of Sorrows

Sermons preached during Lent

AT THE PARISH CHURCH OF

ST. JAMES'S, PICCADILLY

BY

H. G. BONAVIA HUNT

WARDEN AND CHAPLAIN OF TRINITY COLLEGE, LONDON, AND
EVENING PREACHER AT ST. JAMES'S

ἐθεασάμεθα τὴν δόξαν αὐτοῦ

CASSELL & COMPANY, Limited
LONDON, PARIS & NEW YORK
1884

INTRODUCTORY NOTE.

THESE SERMONS were preached at the well-known church of St. James's, Piccadilly, on the Sunday evenings in Lent, 1884. The reader will not, of course, expect so large a subject to be fully treated in six short meditations, the aim having been rather to suggest thought than to supply it.

Easter, 1884.

CONTENTS.

		PAGE
I.	"We Beheld His Glory"	1
II.	"Behold, the Man!"	19
III.	"Behold, your King!"	39
IV.	"Behold, how He loved him"	57
V.	"Behold, a Voice"	75
VI.	"Behold, the Lamb of God!"	95

I.

"We Beheld His Glory."

"Single and clear, not weak or blind,
    The eye must be
To which Thy glory shall an entrance find;
For if Thy chosen ones would gaze on Thee,
    No earthly screen
Between their souls and Thee must intervene."

Lyra Germanica.

I.

"We Beheld His Glory."

(St. John i. 14.)

NIGHT-TIME is not all darkness, any more than day-time—in this country—is unclouded sun. If we step forth from this gas glare* into the outer night, we perceive nothing but blackness in the skies above us; but as we become more and more accustomed to our new surroundings, the expanding pupils of our eyes begin to distinguish the starscape of the heavens, until they take in the whole concave throbbing with myriads of worlds, the panorama of that glorious Universe of life which our own sun shuts up from our sight by day.

Lent-time is not all gloom, any more than night-time is all darkness. Within its protecting

* Sunday Evening, March 2, 1884.

shade the spiritual sight is quickened, its sphere of vision is enlarged; we are enabled to trace more of the great purposes of God in the world, and therefore the better to understand the world itself; we are also permitted to learn more of God as revealed to us in the Person of His Son, and thus to put ourselves into the way of knowing, here in part, and afterwards face to face, what it is to behold the Glory of God.

And so the coming of this new season of Lent invites us to leave for a little space the gay glare of the world's daylight which shuts out the larger universe of God from the soul's view, in order that we may receive the revelation of the Man of Sorrows, with our own eyes steadfastly fixed upon Him, and His eyes gazing deep down into our hearts, stirring within us a keener spiritual consciousness—a consciousness, that is to say, of the matchless grace and tenderness of the Divine Jesus, and of our own utter unworthiness to meet His gaze. For, as we look and look, we grow to understand that light or pomp or majesty is not the only vehicle of God's glory, but everything which has power to move the hearts of men—grief, compassion, forgiveness, sympathy, consolation—all these shining and flashing out like stars in the great firmament of the Gospel dispensation of Incarnate Love.

In this spirit, then, let us contemplate the glories of the Man of Sorrows. Paradox, you will say, always paradox: well, why not? Our Master Himself continually taught by paradox—nay, in all reverence be it spoken, our Lord Himself was the most complete paradox that the world has seen. It was for that reason, principally, that the world could not understand Him—that His fellow-countrymen could not comprehend Him—nay, that His own disciples, one after another, fell away and walked no more with Him. It remains only to such as have the strong spiritual vision of a St. Paul or a St. John to reconcile the two sides of the Paradox, and to feel the whole beauty and perfect unity of Christ in Himself and in His teaching. But although our own spiritual insight may be immeasurably inferior to that possessed by the great Apostles, we are nevertheless privileged to look at the life and character of our Lord through their eyes, and by that means to behold His glory.

Now it would be useless for us to dwell on this subject if we were not fully convinced of its reality—and we must therefore be made to feel the full force of the evidence of St. John. It was the evidence of an eye-witness—the strongest kind of evidence that can be adduced—and it is further emphasised by him in one of his General Epistles—for he speaks of "That which we have heard, which our eyes have seen, and our hands have handled." There is no mistaking the reality of such evidence as this—and if we go back to the passage from which our text is taken, we read: "And the Word was made flesh, and dwelt among us." Yes, St. John had a right to know, if any man had. He had leaned upon the breast of the Saviour of the World, and heard the beating of that pure and suffering heart which was pierced with the transgressions of men. That Presence which St. John beheld and felt was no phantom apparition—it was the true

Shekinah of God tabernacling among men—the glory as of the Only-begotten of the Father. Such was He who dwelt among men, full of grace and truth; and thus St. John recognised the glory of the Godhead in the Manhood of Jesus Christ.

But there was nothing whatever in the outward circumstances of Christ's life to encourage the idea of His being surrounded with glory. If we except the two brief episodes of the Transfiguration and the triumphal entry into Jerusalem, our Lord's earthly career was one of continuous humiliation and disappointment, ending in betrayal and death—despised and rejected—a Man of Sorrows and acquainted with grief. Biblical commentators, treating of this passage in the Gospel, generally point out that St. John in speaking of Christ's glory is alluding to the Transfiguration: there is little doubt of it; but the Apostle in this passage has evidently the whole life—not one small episode of it—before him; the glory of the Agony of the Garden, the glory of the Crown of Thorns, the glory of the Death on the Cross—for that was a glory which no other man could boast—the glory of sinless suffering for the sins of others. All this St. John saw, and those who, with him, were witnesses of the life and death of the Son of Man—that life and that death by which God was made manifest in the flesh. Yes, these witnesses were impressed to the very core of their being with the *reality* of that manifestation—it was the glory of a real bodily presence, a real personal activity, a real sinlessness, a real sympathy, a real humiliation, a real passion, a real sacrifice upon the Cross, a real redemption of a fallen world, a real exaltation of humanity by the uplifting power of a perfect life.

Well, then, we are prepared to receive this testimony of St. John without further question; but that alone does not satisfy us. It will not meet the needs of our own souls to be told that the needs of others have been met and satisfied. Pictures of cooling streams and fountains will not quench a burning thirst, but will rather inflame that thirst. Happy, then, will it be for us if, with our souls athirst for God, the picture of this testimony of the Evangelist shall increase our eagerness to realise it all for ourselves. Believe me, it was for that end that this Gospel was written—that it might excite in us who read it a desire to see, and to be, and to do, those things which will enable us to share in the blessed portion of Christ's true disciples, both here on earth and afterwards in heaven. If, then, we would desire to acquire that spiritual sight which will let into our souls the revelation of the glories of Jesus, we must, in some measure at least, go through the same educating process which St. John and his fellow disciples went through; and the Gospel story shows us the way. Let the Evangelist take us by the hand, and lead us on from step to step of the life of the Man of Sorrows; let us become acquainted with Christ from the cradle to the cross; let us try to know Him thoroughly in every recorded incident—in His dealings with every kind of character, in His conflict with temptations in the wilderness, in His night-long prayer and communion with the Father, in His observance of all the little courtesies of social life, in His forbearance with the infirmities of the weak and erring, in His human affection for those who were near and dear to Him, and His keen solicitude on their behalf—let us try to know Him thoroughly, or as thoroughly as we can, as Man, and by so doing we shall have gone some way towards beholding the glory as of an only begotten of the Father, to which St. John, in our text, has testified. We shall then have arrived at the position of being spectators of the life of the Son of Man.

But we must needs go a step higher than this, otherwise we shall get no nearer than Balaam of old did, who beheld Him, but not nigh, or those spectators upon Golgotha, who seeing the Lord Jesus on the cross smote their breasts and returned to their darkened homes. If we would seek to share in the happy experiences of St. John we must set about cultivating a habit of close personal contact with Jesus. The disciple whom Jesus loved leaned on His breast at supper, and this act itself is simply significant of the personal relationship which existed between the disciple and his Lord — the outward position, that is to say, was nothing in itself unless it showed the closeness of spiritual communion— that there was so compact a bond that nothing must be suffered to come between them. Tell me, now, was it possible to be so near to Jesus without receiving greater spiritual enlightenment and joy? Remember that the scroll of the Revelation was unrolled to us by the hand of St. John the Divine, and let us recognise that whosoever leans on Jesus' breast is very, very near to the glory and the bliss of heaven. And recognising this, let us also grasp a truth which should afford us encouragement and help in our aspirations after the divine life — namely, that the same measure of spiritual communion is open to every disciple of the Lord Jesus now; that although He is not with us in the flesh, the conditions of spiritual fellowship enjoyed by St. John are in nowise altered; that the same soul enlightenment and heart comfort may be realised by ourselves if only we will put ourselves into the right way of attaining to a habit of constant communication with the divine source of every good and perfect gift. And that communication, that communion, how is it to be maintained? Not simply by coming to church at certain intervals; not simply by going through the formulæ of home devotions at set hours. The performance of these religious duties should be regarded as the natural outcome of the inner life, a healthy expression of the spiritual force within us. They may and do quicken the pulses of the soul, but they will never keep these pulses going steadily, regularly, firmly, from moment to moment of our lives. No, we cannot secure the culture of our souls by the mere forcing apparatus of sermons, litanies, and books of devotion. We must spiritually bring ourselves to the side of Jesus at every available moment by day or night. When we sit down to our work let us have Jesus for our companion; when we walk in the busy streets let us still commune with Him in our hearts, recalling all that He has said to His disciples of old, and applying His counsels and warnings, His encouragements and endearments, to ourselves, as, indeed, He intended we should do; let us sedulously, I say, cultivate this habit of mind, devote ourselves to this culture of soul, and we shall surely get to know what it is to lean with St. John upon the breast of Jesus, and behold the glory of the Only-begotten beaming upon us from the face of the Man of Sorrows.

And what is to be the effect of this upon you and me? Is the result to be limited to a vague something in the far-off future—a happiness into which we cannot enter in this life? Not so; the effect on our life and character is to be a present one, in earnest of what we are to see and know and enjoy hereafter. The effect of constant communion or communication with the Divine Jesus is similar to that which comes of constant intercourse with any character or presence of force superior to our own. If we look at children—they are our miniature selves—we shall see that they have the gift of unconscious imitation—their voices, their gestures, their talk, their likes and dislikes, are all more or less modelled upon those of their parents or others having the constant guardianship of them; and that same imitative faculty remains in them through life, though showing itself in different forms at different periods of life. The glory which men saw upon the face of Moses when he came down from the Mount, was surely meant to teach us that contact with Divine influences—nay, more precisely, with the Divine Being—is followed by exactly similar results; that you cannot live in the atmosphere of the Godhead without some of that glory being reflected in yourself, and to be seen in your own face by others; that you cannot look into the face of Jesus without receiving upon yourself the impress—in some far-off feeble way—but yet the positive impression of His image and likeness; and that the natural result in you of beholding His glory is to make you more and more like Him in all His manliness as perfect Man.

"Yes, but *cui bono*—what is the good of it

all?" some will ask. "If we would share His mind and heart, we must in some measure be prepared to behold His sorrow, to share in His bitter experiences of the world that crucified Him. For the life of Christ was a life of suffering, a life altogether and most obstinately misunderstood, a life ending in a cruel death. We can never bring ourselves to live such a life." There is no need to say so. We never can live His life as He lived it. But we can try to live upon the plan of life He has laid down for us. The question is, What other kind of living shall we choose? The world's way? Those who have gone the whole length of it turn round and tell us that it is disgusting and disappointing in the extreme. "The world passeth away, and the lust thereof." The glory of the world, like some gorgeous display of fireworks, flashes and dances before the eyes for a moment, and then leaves as it were a greater darkness. Such is the glory which the worldling loves to behold, and we answer him back, *cui bono*—what avails it? And in this rejoinder a cold hard voice chimes in with ours—that of the cynic. But let us not be beguiled into joining hands with him, for though he professes contempt of the worldling the two have very much in common. The cynic's way is no path for us to tread who value sympathy and comfort. Let all those who are in trouble, sorrow, need, sickness, or any other adversity, forbear to grasp the cynic's hand, for in it they will find no more response than in the hand of the dead. And why? because he places himself on a pedestal of his own, apart from his brother men; he steels his own heart against sorrow or trial, no tender emotion of love or pity moves his breast; he is a man of rebuffs, a moral iceberg, a master of sneers; his glory at the most is the momentary flash of the lightning, which spends itself by scathing and killing where it falls. No, we recoil with horror from the cynic's way; we turn with pity from the worldling's way; and more and more strongly we feel it borne in upon us that the way of Christ is, after all, the way for us, that the way of the Cross is the only way of happiness, and of that peace which passeth understanding and lasts for ever and ever.

We shall learn, then, during the blessed season on which we have now entered, to use its opportunities for quickening and widening our spiritual sight, so that we may realise, as we never realised before, the fulness of the glory of the Man of Sorrows; not for the mere purpose of emotional contemplation, but also and above all that we may model our lives upon that Master Life; receiving upon our souls the impress of His Divine Image; daily striving to cling closer and closer to Him; walking with Him in the rocky path of mortification and self-sacrifice; beholding Him in the Majesty of His sorrow, that we may see, and know, and in ourselves exemplify, the exceeding riches of His glory.

II.

"Behold, the Man!"

" So knowing all God's worship to be Thine,
  We strain our souls to praise Thee, Light of Light;
But Thou art not less human than Divine—
  Thy Manhood claims its right.

          *   *   *   *   *   *

" Thou took'st on Thee this flesh and soul of ours,
  And they by that assumption glorified,
And now enriched with yet sublimer powers,
  For ever Thine abide."

William Bright.

II.

"Behold, the Man!"

(St. John xix. 5.)

THERE are those amongst us, probably, who can call to mind at least one occasion when some apparently trivial remark, forgotten for the time as soon as spoken, has been followed by an incident—perhaps the death of a friend, or some other momentous episode in one's life—which has recalled the words with startling vividness, investing them with the character of an unconscious prophecy. "I little thought," is the common exclamation in such cases, "that those words of mine had so much meaning in them, or that they were to be so amply, so literally fulfilled."

In like manner, many historic sayings which have come down to us have acquired their significance in the after-glow cast upon them by great events. They have mostly been uttered on the spur of the moment—almost involuntarily—and though creating but little impression at the time, have become immortal by the force of some mighty crisis in the affairs of a nation or the fortunes of a dynasty.

Sometimes the speaker is a person of genius and world-wide repute; but more often this is not the case. Take the scene presented to us in the Gospel. Who among the crowd began the awful, the prophetic vociferation—" His blood be on us, and on our children "—which now we know to be so full of solemn import? A rash retort upon the disclaimer of the Roman judge, snapped out by some frenzied man, and caught up by an excited rabble, the majority of them hardly conscious of what they were saying—that is all. There is no knowing what hasty words of ours may, in spite of ourselves, acquire a baleful immortality.

Little thought Pontius Pilate, the petty governor of a conquered province, that his name was to be a familiar one in the mouths of millions, and for so long as the world should last, or that his sayings and doings at that dread scene of the trial of our Lord were to assume a magnitude of importance far greater than the words and deeds of all the Cæsars. When Pilate exclaimed, "Behold, the Man!" he was unconscious that he was uttering an immortal sentence, a stupendous truth; he was simply struck with the unusual aspect of the Accused One as He stood before His judge fresh from the scourgings and the insults of the soldiers, the wan face sprinkled with the blood-drops from the crown of thorns; meek, yet full of dignity, bowed and yet unshrinking, the form scantly covered with the purple of mock royalty—all this cruel treatment of the person of Jesus seemed the more barbarous from its unwonted incongruity, so that Pilate could only ejaculate his involuntary admiration of the majestic Being who stood before him. Look, what a man! Here is, indeed, a man above other men. Such was the tribute wrung from the Procurator of Judea, a weak and despicable creature, unequal to the courage of his own convictions, unworthy the noble name of Roman : and in his own mouth the confession was worth little ; but the occasion stamped upon it the seal of immortality ; it has become a watchword of Christianity ; the great fact it embodies is one of the glories of the Man of Sorrows.

In our last meditation we strove to learn to behold the glory of Him who dwelt among us, and we found that St. John attained to that spiritual enlightenment by means of his knowledge of Christ as man. And we cannot do better than continue to follow the lead of St. John, who, in placing on record the Ecce Homo of Pilate, again directs our attention to the manhood of Jesus Christ our Lord.

Now, it seems to me that there is an unconscious tendency amongst Christians to accentuate the doctrine of the Divine Nature of our Lord so strongly as to enfeeble their grasp of the co-ordinate fact of His Human Nature. This is due, no doubt, to the constant attacks of schismatics, past and present, against the divinity of Christ ; but, depend upon it, while laying every stress upon this vital doctrine of His divinity, we shall lose a great deal if we fail to realise in its fullest extent the complete humanity of our blessed Saviour—that while He is God with us He is none the less Man with us; that while He manifests God to man, He represents man to God, being bone of our bone and flesh of our flesh. There is little danger in the present of any revival of the ancient Docetic heresy—that our Saviour's form was but a mere appearance; but there is always need to guard against the feeling that in His humanity there was hardly anything in common with ours besides the bodily frame. His was a human soul as well as a human body. As a man He was precisely what Adam was as God first created him, and before he fell into sin. Christ was the second Adam. The first Adam was tempted, and sinned; the second Adam was tempted, and remained pure. That purity exalted His manhood immeasurably above the level of sinful humanity, yet it did not obliterate His manhood, but glorified it—made His manhood more perfect and more complete than that of any other man on earth. In Jesus Christ we see man as God made him; in mankind we see man as the devil has marred him.

If we would wish to realise what Adam was before the Fall, and what in consequence we might have been but for that Fall, we need only study the character of Christ as man, as presented to us in the Gospels. But we must also take note of this all-important difference between the environment of the first Adam and that of the second Adam. The first Adam entered upon a sinless world; the first stain upon it was man's transgression. The second Adam came into a world foul to the core with sin, reeking with every kind of abominable iniquity. He was fashioned like unto ourselves—that is, in the flesh; and as a Man of Sorrows He was more in sympathy with us as man is now constituted after the deteriorating effect of ages upon ages of sin committed by the fathers and visited upon the children. He was a Man born into an old, decrepit, sin-weakened race. And He was continually assailed by the Tempter, in one form or another.

Had He not been accessible to temptation, Satan could not have tempted Him: had He not felt the attack, where would have been the glory of His lifelong triumph over temptation?

Behold Him, then, the Tempted Man, "in all points tempted like as we are, yet without sin." His sinlessness was no outer panoply of steel which shielded Him from the deadly brunt of conflict with the Evil One. Every dart went home, bringing with it quivering pain. But the fount of purity within was not to be contaminated; it rejected the poison of the dart, which had power to inflict the sting of horror, yet in nowise to vitiate the inner life or to mar the beauty of that perfect holiness. Yes, the brunt and buffet of temptation caused intense suffering to the Man of Sorrows, in fulfilment of the prophecy made to the Serpent in the Garden at the time of man's transgression. It was because Jesus was so perfectly pure, while so thoroughly a man, that He suffered so keenly. And this being so, we shall learn that in proportion to the vigour of our spiritual health will be the intensity of our sufferings in the struggle with temptation.

The greatest danger to our bodies is the *unfelt* harm. If the piercing of the outer flesh were to cause no sensation of pain, some vital part might be reached without warning. Physical pain, then, is a great safeguard of our bodies. So is it with the inner life. The impact of sin, if it cause us no pain, no shrinking, is fraught with deadly peril. But if when we feel its smarting touch we recoil with horror, and cry out, " Lord! help me," we are safe. To a similar effect speaks the good Saint Francis of Sales. " Though a temptation," he says, "to any sin whatsoever, should last during life, it would never render us displeasing to the Divine Majesty, provided we took no pleasure in it, and did not yield our consent to it. The reason is, because in temptation we do not act, but endure; and as in this we take no pleasure, so we cannot incur any guilt. St. Paul suffered a long time the temptations of the flesh, and yet so far was he from being displeasing to God on that account, that God, on the contrary, was glorified thereby." And so, taking up the argument of St. Francis, and applying it to the Great Exemplar of St. Paul and of all mankind, we see how God was glorified in the Temptation of the Man Christ Jesus, who, being without sin, suffered and endured infinitely more than sinful man is capable of by reason of the atrophy which has deadened the finer parts of his moral being.

Again, we must not forget to notice that the greater the prominence of the individual, and the more he stands out from his fellow-men, the more liable he is to the assaults of the Tempter. Now people in a humble condition of life are very prone to think that the higher the station of a man, and the more free he is from what we may call the petty trials of life, the fewer the temptations that assail him. Let us assure such that the converse of this is the case. To widen the environment of the individual, is to multiply opportunities for attack upon him. The bird that flies is in more instant and constant peril of its life than the mole which burrows in the ground. The more exalted, therefore, that a man's position is, the more refined his nature, the more numerous and subtle become the sources of temptation. And so, Christ, standing alone among men in His majestic sinlessness, called into play every possible resource of the Tempter—temptations were presented to Him that we know nothing of, because we are not pure enough to feel them. They pierced every fibre of his sensitive Being, causing an agony which, when the conflict was over and the victory won, drew down the very Angels of God from heaven to minister unto Him. Behold, the Man!

And we shall greatly add to our knowledge of Christ as a Man if we behold Him, The Praying Man. I find that time will not permit me to dwell proportionately on this part of my subject, but there is just one point I should like to present to your view, namely, that the Divine Jesus cannot have prayed otherwise than as a Man. As God He had no need to pray, to petition for anything, to aspire to anything. He and the Father were one then—as now—as always. So that when Christ prayed He by that act distinguished His Manhood, so to speak, from His Godhead, and for the time felt as entirely and exclusively Man, asking for strength to bear the burden of trial and the Cross; praying that God's will might be done. Now Christ had all the instincts of. Manhood in a perfect degree, by reason of His sinlessness; and when He prayed He was simply exercising the instinct within Him in the same natural way that the bird of the air, having wings, uses them to fly; or the fish of the sea, having fins, uses them in the water. If the instinct of prayer in a man is dulled or dormant, it is only a sign that the higher functions of his nature are blunted and deadened—that he does not live the full life of which man is capable, the life of loving contact with his Maker. Christ, then, was a Man of Prayer because He was every whit a Man: and the more a man cultivates this grand instinct of Prayer, the more perfect will his own manhood be—the nearer will he attain to the perfect stature of the Man Christ Jesus.

The good Bishop Porteous, preaching in this

church one Lent, at the beginning of this century, remarked that "Our Lord did not pretend to that unfeeling heroism, that total insensibility to pain and affliction, which some of the ancient philosophers affected. On the contrary, in His human nature He felt like a man; He felt the weight of His own sorrows, and dropped the tear of sympathy for those of others. To those, therefore, who are oppressed and bowed down (as the best of men sometimes are) with a load of grief—who find, as the Psalmist expresses it, "their flesh and their heart failing," and their spirits sinking within them, it must be a most reviving consideration to reflect that in this state even of extreme depression, there is no guilt; that it is no mark of God's displeasure; that even His beloved Son was no stranger to it; that He was a Man of Sorrows and well acquainted with grief; that therefore He is not a hard, unfeeling, obdurate Master, who cannot be touched with our infirmities, but one who was in all things tried and afflicted as we are, yet without sin. He knows what sorrow is; He knows how hard it sometimes presses, even on the firmest minds, and He will not fail to extend that relief to others, for which even He himself applied with so much fervency to the Father of all."

Among the many other standpoints from which we may contemplate the glories of Christ as a man, let us take only one more. Let us behold Him, The Dying Man. As in His Godhead He could not die, surely it was as very man that He cried—" Father, into Thy hands I commend my spirit!" The last flicker of the lamp of His human life, the last sigh of His departing breath, were expended in those words of loving, trustful peace. And in this act He surely taught us that better than all the masses for the dead is it for a man to breathe into the ear of God his own Requiem, his own sweet *Nunc Dimittis.* He taught us, too, that to have lived well is to die well; that whatever the accidents of death, however sad in themselves, however heartrending, the dews of death hang lightly on the brow of a man whose heart is at one with the Father. Yes, my brethren, the Christian's death is the consummation, the crown of his manhood. For he has not done with trying to fashion himself after the pattern of his Lord and Master, until he has tried to die as Jesus died.

Well, then, I have endeavoured to bring before you, so far as may be within the limits of a brief meditation, one or two lights in which we may behold our Saviour as a man. You will notice that throughout it has been impossible to forget that He is God as well as Man—for the more we study Him as man, the nearer we get to behold His divine glory, as St. John did—and so long as we keep within sight of that fundamental truth we cannot go far astray. But let us beware of divorcing His human from His divine nature, as those do who approach the subject in a purely critical and speculative spirit. These end by falling into rhapsodies of admiration which are repulsive to the spiritual sense. Mere philosophical admiration is insulting to the character of Him who commands the fervent adoration, the ceaseless devotion and worship of our hearts. For Jesus, as man, is no mere character in history. He became man to die for us; He became man to show us how both to live and to die; nor did He cease to be man when He died on Calvary. He rose from the dead as man; He ascended into heaven as man —He is still the man Christ Jesus; our High Priest, making intercession for us.

"No man" saith God, "can see my face and live." But in the fulness of time, and in the depth of His wondrous mercy, God sent forth His Son, made in the likeness of men, that we beholding Him as man, might be enabled to see as in a glass the Glory of God. "He that hath seen me," saith Christ, "hath seen the Father." Behold, then, the Man! "No," say the wise men of this world, "we decline to see anything beyond what we are able to formulate of our own philosophy." And so they go on theorising, formulating, straining after they know not what. Agnosticism has made a bold flight of it, and has come down again like a spent rocket. Another development of so-called free thought is the adoration of a kind of fetish under the name of "Humanity;" but what these philosophical minds mean that we shall include in the term is not very clear. We only know that humanity as we see it in the world, as we see it in ourselves, is full of sin unto death, a mass of corruption, a pitiable spectacle of tottering weakness. But when in defence of their curious religion they tell us, " You can have no religion without kinship, sympathy, relation of some human kind between the believer, worshipper, servant, and the object of his belief, worship, and service,"* we can only answer that they are unconsciously asking for that very boon which they are doggedly turning their backs upon. Why, here, in the person of Christ, is all that their hearts are yearning for. What nearer and dearer kinship, what more perfect sympathy, what human relationship more precious can mortal find than in Him that sticketh closer than a brother? Come, then, all ye wandering waifs and strays of poor humanity; come, ye faltering, blundering, blinded leaders of the blind; and come, too, ye anxious seekers after the higher truth and the better life; come, ye that have sinned and suffered, and have

* *Nineteenth Century*, No. 85, p. 505.

found no pity nor hope in the world; come, ye that are friendless and forsaken, and pining for sympathy and love; come hither and behold the Man who will give you all that you need—light, and life, and healing, and sympathy, and hope, and joy unspeakable! In the hour of temptation He will stand by and strengthen you; in the hour of prayer He will take you by the hand and link you thus with your God; in the hour of death, when the dread loneliness comes upon you, and all the world has faded from your sight, when your loved ones of earth can walk no further with you into the Valley, when you have lost touch of them, and can no longer feel the farewell kiss—then you will feel the arms of Jesus strong and loving round about you, and your head will be pillowed upon the breast of His everlasting love.

III.

"Behold, your King!"

> "Hath He diadem as Monarch
> That His brow adorns?
> Yea, a Crown, in very surety,
> But of thorns."
>
> — *J. M. Neale.*

III.

"Behold, your King!"
(ST. JOHN xix. 14.)

HERE we see Christ proclaimed King of the Jews by the official representative of Tiberius Cæsar, the great autocrat and king-maker of the world.

Some have supposed that Pilate made this proclamation in jest, in derision of Jesus, and in mocking allusion to the crown of thorns and the purple robe which the common soldiers had put upon Jesus after the scourging. But this supposition is hardly in keeping with the words and actions of Pilate at this later stage of the trial. His great anxiety to release the prisoner would not allow of a jest at His expense, though he might well have expressed his scorn of the rabble who besieged the courtyard of his palace.

And had the people suddenly changed, as mobs have been known to change, their cry—had they taken Pilate at his word, our Lord might have been carried by popular acclaim to the throne of Judea at the suggestion of the Roman Governor; and Pilate momentarily ran that risk. But this was not to be. Our Lord, whose Kingdom was not of this world, had already passed through this temptation, and it was not now to be repeated. Prophecy had been fulfilled. The sceptre had finally departed from Judah, by the death many years before of Herod the Great— that Herod to whom the birth of Christ had been announced by the Magi, as the birth of the rightful King of the Jews. Herod had evidently been aware that lineal descendants of the House of David were possibly living: and the result of his inquiries, into the details of which the Evangelist does not consider it necessary to enter, led to the massacre of the infant children of Bethlehem—one of the many horrors of that cruel reign.

But let us now look a little more closely at

the scene presented to us in the Gospel story. Pilate, deeply inpressed not only with the pathetic appearance of our Blessed Saviour—so unlike the dogged, sullen, and vicious bearing of other criminals with whom he was accustomed to deal—but also with the divine dignity and awful import of His replies to the questions put to Him, goes out once more to the Jews, and bids them behold their King. The crowd, exasperated at this speech, which they regard in the light of a contemptuous taunt (for it must be remembered that Jesus is still arrayed in the mock purple, with the crown of thorns upon His brow), cry out, " Away with Him! Crucify, crucify Him!" "What!" said Pilate, "crucify your King?" "We have no king but Cæsar," is the reply—they will say anything, no matter how distasteful to their national pride, anything to get rid of the present object of their frantic hatred. Then comes a cunning retort upon Pilate, evidently suggested by the more astute among the ringleaders of the mob—"If thou let this Man go, thou art not Cæsar's friend."

This was the shaft that struck. Pilate, as they well knew, dared not risk an accusation of this kind being sent to Rome. He had already suffered some disagreeable experiences with the people of Judea; and a further representation, especially one affecting the sovereign prerogatives of Cæsar himself, would infallibly cost him his office, if not more. So under the pressure of an impatient and threatening multitude, he gave way; and Christ, the true King of the Jews, was given up to be crucified—" crucified for us, under Pontius Pilate."

The inconsistency of the Jews on this occasion was characteristic in the extreme. Possessed with the one absorbing idea of the hour—a thirst for the life of Him who all His life had been their staunchest Friend, their boldest advocate against the unrighteous oppression of their spiritual masters, they were oblivious of all argument, and indeed of their own words and actions from moment to moment. When asked whom they would have released unto them in customary honour of their great Feast of the Passover, they chose a rebel and a shedder of blood, one who had set at naught the laws of God and man. Next they cried out that they would have no king but Cæsar—whose authority, as represented in that province, had been defied by the very man they asked to have released. They themselves had always been ready for revolt—every political dreamer and schemer, as their history shows, found in them a ready tool to his hand. Still more remarkable was the inconsistency of their attitude towards Christ Himself. Not many months back the people had wanted to make Him their King; and indeed, as we are told, would have taken Him by force for that purpose, but that He eluded them. Only a day or two before the trial they had cried, " Hosanna to the Son of David!" and invoked blessings upon Him who came in the Name of the Lord—and Pilate must have known of this. It is now Pilate's turn to say to them, " Behold, your King!" His words under all these circumstances had a bitter sting for them which might well goad them to madness. And though he basely yielded to their clamour, Pilate would not spare them the reproach of ingratitude to One who had been their Benefactor and Friend, the accusation of disloyalty to One who by right of descent and according to their own laws was their King. "This is Jesus, the King of the Jews," was the writing upon the Cross, and though they implored him to change the wording of it, Pilate remained firm in this, the only point from which he would not swerve.

Truly spoke Christ our Lord when He said, "My Kingdom is not of this world." For the earthly coronation of Christ was a Crown of Thorns; His enthronement was the exaltation of the Cross; His Chief Council of State, the Apostles, had—with the sole exception of the writer of this Gospel—forsaken Him and fled; His Treasurer had sold Him to His enemies for thirty pieces of silver; and yet that coronation, that enthronement, was the most memorable ceremony, the most glorious inauguration that this world has seen. The millions who in ages past have done homage to the Cæsars of the earth, have been immeasurably outnumbered by the myriads who have bent the knee before the King upon the Cross. All the brightest genius of the world has been dedicated to the portrayal of that His "reigning from the Tree:" poet, painter, sculptor, and musician, each has consecrated his highest work to the celebration of this glory of the Man of Sorrows; each with his own peculiar eloquence, whether by the rolling cadence of solemn verse, or by no less speaking canvas or by marble, or by the sweetest sadness of passion-music — has said, "Behold, your King!" And more than all, Apostle, Evangelist, Martyr, Confessor—in a word, the voice of the Church of the living God—has reiterated the proclamation in the ears of mankind from age to age; and although many, alas! have wagged their heads and passed by unheeding, no generation has been lacking in those who have meekly knelt with St. John and the three Marys before the King of kings and Lord of lords.

But for ourselves, who have heard Christ proclaimed King of the Jews—King, that is to say, of all who are of the true Israel of God—how do we receive that proclamation?

Those amongst whom Christ is proclaimed may be classed in four groups—those who openly renounce His allegiance, and are all for Cæsar; those who profess allegiance to Christ, but really serve Cæsar; those who strive with all their might to serve both together; and, lastly, those who try to serve Christ alone, at whatever cost and risk.

Those of the first group are easily discoverable. They announce themselves everywhere with unblushing candour, whether by word or by action; there is no need for me to describe either. You have only to step out of this church to pass multitudes of such within a minute. There are hundreds of men and women you meet within a few yards of this place—in Piccadilly, in the Haymarket, in Regent Street—who are as palpably the creatures of this world's vanities and lusts as though they had the name of Cæsar written in their foreheads. Some bear marks of the highest respectability—others of the deepest degradation. If you were to say to any of them this Lent, "Behold, your King!" they would frankly tell you in their own fashion that they had no King but Cæsar, and would not trouble themselves about any one else at present. Meantime, are any of these subjects of Cæsar happy or at peace? Look at their faces for answer. There is no sign of rest there. "There is no peace, saith my God, to the wicked." Day after day they re-enact in their lives the awful tragedy of Golgotha—they crucify their King; some of malice aforethought, others in mere heedlessness—for they that crucify their King to-day are as variously constituted as the crowd who raved in the outer court of Pilate's judgment hall. It was for all these, now living as well as passed away, that Jesus prayed, "Father, forgive them, for they know not what they do!" Yes, and if all the voices of earth were hushed about us at this moment, we should hear that calm and all-prevailing voice of loving intercession, pleading still for them and for us.

The second group—those who profess the

service of the true King while remaining the servants of Cæsar, are the King's enemies who have gotten within the camp. They wear all the outward badges of the King's service; in appearance they are not to be distinguished from the true soldiers of the Cross. Nay, at a glance one might excusably deem them to be the flower and strength of that noble army, they march along so bravely beneath the Royal banners. If there should be any signs of external onslaught upon the Church Militant, their voices are loudest against the designs of the invader. They are the stalwart heroes of the parade. When it comes to the steady, patient hand-to-hand conflict, when the struggle is at the fiercest, you look around you for encouragement from those brave comrades— they are gone from your side. At length you find them, like Balaam of old, fighting in the ranks of the Lord's enemies. The sin of such as these is not the sin of Pilate. It is far worse. It is the hateful crime of Iscariot, who brake bread with his Master in the pledge of close communion, of inviolable fidelity, and then went out and sold

Him to His murderers. Jesus prayed for the savage horde that hounded Him to death: but there is no record of any prayer for Judas. The plea, "They know not what they do!" could hardly have been applied to him, or such as he. There is sin which cannot be forgiven, not because of any limit to the love of God, but because it is the result of a nature in essence Satanic, and therefore beyond the conditions which lead to repentance.

The third group—a far larger one—consists of those who try to reap the advantages of both services. Those who belong to this class may be familiarly described as paying court to Cæsar on week-days and to Christ on Sundays. Not that they are in the habit of admitting to themselves this process of double dealing with their own souls. On Sundays, and at special seasons such as Advent or Lent, they are most earnest—or believe themselves so to be—in their loyal adherence to the authority of Christ the King. If in their hearing others were to disavow that authority, the announcement would cause them dismay and abhorrence. In the public worship of the Church, in the private devotions of the home, they proclaim the Kingship of Christ with no faltering voice; in any attack of the Evil One or of his agents upon the Kingdom of Christ on earth, they will be ready and true up to a given point. But let any real struggle ensue, in which the strain is placed upon their own line in the battle's front, and we then find that they are but soldiers of straw. In plain truth, they are only half-hearted servants of our King; they are really hankering after the service of Cæsar; and hope to secure their citizenship in the heavenly Kingdom by formally pledging themselves to the service of Christ, and performing certain regulation duties in a dry, cold, almost heartless fashion. But our King will not accept such service at our hands. He does not value our homage one whit except so far as it represents the moving love of our hearts, the active gratitude of our lives. "No man can serve two masters," saith Christ. "Ye cannot serve God and mammon." For all the real hold that your loyalty has upon you, ye might be deserters, open and self-acknowledged. Deserters indeed ye are already, for your hearts are really with the Cæsar of this world, whose pay ye are in part receiving out of the fleeting and unsatisfying pleasures of the present life.

The last group—those who are wholly devoted to their sovereign Lord—may be small comparatively, but it is numerically larger than many are apt to think. They do not strive nor cry, nor lift up their voice in the streets, any more than the great Master did, and hence the majority of them are unnoticed by their brethren. Their speech is quiet, their actions are unobtrusive, and yet both by speech and by action they proclaim, far more effectually than the world supposes or they themselves may be conscious of, the Kingdom of their Lord upon the earth. Their whole life is a practical treatise of the Imitation of Christ—following afar off, as it must needs be, but still following, imitating; their eyes ever fixed upon the Man of Sorrows reigning upon the Cross. There is always a brighter and a purer light in the eye that looks upward; this is so even in the flesh; and when the eye of the soul is raised to the dying Saviour's face as it bends forward from the height of the Cross, it is the light of the Godhead, of perfect love and purity, that shines forth reflected upon the retina of the spiritual vision. These behold their King.

Were we to visit some distant country, whose inhabitants had been delivered from the tyranny of a grinding despot, or from the overrunning of hordes of robbers and freebooters, we should probably find very little difference in the people as we met them in the streets, absorbed in their various occupations; but let us get to know them individually, and see them in their homes, and we shall find a glow of happiness, an atmosphere of restfulness, to which they were strangers in the time of their oppression, although belike they had their carnival times of feasting and revelry and superficial rejoicings. And so it is, that while they raise no feverish stir about them, and wear no gay trappings of the carnival, you may know the subjects of our King by the light which shines in their lives. And if you get to know them well, and to see them in the walk of their daily round, you will learn that they, too, know what it is to have been delivered from the tyranny of Cæsar, from the overrunning of evil thoughts and passions that steal and defile the priceless treasures of the soul; they know that their true King is no hard despot, but a loving sympathising Brother; they know that He suffered for their sakes far more than words can tell or heart can fathom; and they know that after the little they gladly suffer with Him and for His sake on earth, they shall reign together with Him in the Kingdom of His glory.

Brethren, behold your King! One day you must behold Him in His awful majesty, coming in the clouds of heaven. He gave His word for this to His accusers, and He will keep that word with them and you. But if you will draw near to Him now as He hangs upon the cross, if you will take your pledge of fealty, and enthrone Him in your hearts and lives, you shall not fear to meet Him then, for He knoweth them that are His, and will give them to share His throne and His glory in the life to come.

IV.

Behold, how He loved him.

"Ah, Love of God, if greater love than this
  Hath no man, that a man die for his friend;
 And if such love of love Thine own Love is,
  Plead with Thyself, with me, before the end."

Christina Rossetti.

IV.

"Behold, how He loved him."

(St. John xi. 36.)

THAT the love of Jesus is human as well as divine we all acknowledge—in theory. Few amongst us realise it in our lives as we might, because we fail to distinguish between the sympathetic love of our Elder Brother and the compassionate love of the Son of God. And we can only properly realise the value of this golden attribute of our Saviour's Manhood, by cherishing it as one of the inherent beauties of His perfect humanity, by extolling it as one of the brightest glories of the Man of Sorrows.

We cannot afford, my brethren, to dispense with any portion of that priceless boon which God gave to us when He sent His Only-begotten Son into the world made in the likeness of men.

And this is why in the present series of meditations I have ventured to insist again and again upon the thoroughly human character of Christ, without for one moment losing sight of His perfect Godhead.

And the more we give ourselves up to the contemplation of the human tenderness of the Divine Jesus, so much the more closely shall we feel ourselves drawn to Him. If His disciples felt this strong personal attraction to Him both while He was with them in the world and after He had left them to go to the Father—may not we? He is the same Man Christ Jesus that He was when in the world; His human heart still beats for His loving and loved disciples.

There was nothing distant or cold in the individual affections of Jesus. His love was no mere logical demonstration of a philosophical system—no mere item in a code of morals. True it was both these in a sense, but it was infinitely more: it was the mainspring of His dealings with those around Him—an instinct of His perfect Manhood which showed itself at the most trying crisis of His earthly career. Yes! even amidst the awful agonies of the Cross, when the great act of redemption was being consummated in the sight of God and man, He, the central figure of the Universe, must needs think of His mother, committing her to the tender guardianship of the only friend who stood by Him to the end. And that friend—the disciple whom Jesus loved—we know that there was a special attachment, a particular personal affection—between St. John and his Lord, to which the Evangelist more than once calls our attention. We thus learn that while our Saviour loved the whole world, loved even His enemies, loved the vilest sinners as apart from their wrong-doings, yearned over His fellow-countrymen, and deeply cherished the love of His disciples, He had at the same time an inner sanctuary in His human heart for His relatives and intimate friends. Of the twelve whom He called to be His chief disciples, the Apostles Peter, James, and John were singled out to accompany Him to the Mount of Transfiguration and to other scenes of special import. Speaking familiarly, He took these three more into his confidence than all the rest, and of the three St. John stood first in His personal regard. Now we often hear it said—as though it were a thing to boast of—we often hear persons proclaim aloud that they have no preferences, and that they love everybody alike. These good people seem to imagine that to own a preference is to confess a weakness. Nay, but is it not rather a confession of dryness of heart, of poverty of affection, when your love is spread, as it were, in one dead level within an even radius around you, and you have no further to spare above and beyond for those who by affinity of blood or kinship of mind and heart would fain draw upon your store? Not in this wise, my brethren, speaketh the Gospel record of Christ; on the contrary, we find abundant evidence of His especial human friendships, and of that warmth of heart which is known amongst ourselves as an "affectionate disposition." Yes, the Blessed Lord Jesus had His individual preferences, because out of the depths of His all-loving heart there was not only enough love to embrace the whole world, but ever fresh fountains of affection for those who shared His daily life and ate with Him their daily bread, sweetened past expression with the manly love of a Perfect Man.

Does any one here recoil from this thought as I have ventured to put it to you? Far be it from any of us to treat the most sacred of all subjects with needless and jarring familiarity; but it would be well for us to remember at the same time that it is one of the subtle temptations of Satan—one of the cunning devices which he employs against Christians—to make the suggestion or reproach of want of due reverence a means of keeping us at a distance from our beloved Saviour. Oh, blessed familiarity, for which no doubt many would have reproved St. John, who dared to lean his head upon that most sacred breast, which held human affection enough and to spare, not only for him but for you!

And so, to proceed, we will dare to take hold upon Christ as our best Human Friend as well as our Divine Benefactor, to look upon Him as the ideal Man, our highest model of manliness. Think of that, young lads, when you are incited to speak lightly of home and parents, and remember that the truest manliness is to love and reverence them, as Christ loved and revered His mother, remaining subject unto her and supporting her with the labour of His hands at home until He began to be about thirty years of age. Think of that, grown men of the world, when the career you have chosen appears to demand so much devotion that you cannot spare a corner of your heart for the claims and the solace of private friendship; and remember that He who had an immeasurably higher and more engrossing life-work than you, could spare the time to share the social intercourse of those about Him, and to take His accustomed place in the home of Lazarus and his sisters Mary and Martha, to receive their little confidences and to soothe their little afflictions, as well as to comfort them in their greater trials.

In that greatest, sharpest trial of all — that trial of faith and of patience—which visited the peaceful home in Bethany, Christ stands forth preeminently as the Friend of the bereaved family. He goes to the grave of His beloved Lazarus, weeping in sympathy for the grief of the two chief mourners. When, a few days before, the sisters sent Him their message, "Lord, he whom Thou lovest is sick," He had appeared to neglect that call upon His affection. As hour after hour passed by, and the two heartbroken sisters took it in turns to watch and to wait, one by the bedside of their brother, while the other strained her eyes and ears for the first glimpse and sound of the coming of their Friend, their faith, especially that of the naturally impatient Martha, must have been sorely tried. It was so unlike Him! they must have thought. It was contrary to all they knew of Him, that He should share the happiness of His friends and leave them to grapple with their trouble alone. And we, too, cannot but feel and know, as they afterwards knew, that but for the higher purpose which the Saviour had in view He would have come to their aid before even the message had left their

F

lips. Yes, Lazarus, the beloved of Jesus, must die, that in him mankind should see the glory of God as manifested by Christ in the power of the resurrection from the dead. The first greeting of Jesus to Martha was, "Thy brother shall rise again." She had not long now to wait before those words had for her a present force and life which should open to her a full revelation of joy. But ere He stretched forth the mighty hand of God, they saw Him for the moment as all in all their Friend; they saw the tears of Jesus being shed for them. And the neighbours, who had come in true neighbourly fashion to mourn with the bereaved, paused in their own kindly demonstrations of sorrow to exclaim, "Behold, how He must have loved him!"

O blessed Sympathy, divine daughter of the Infinite Love, how sweet a gift thou art to a world of sorrow and pain! Thy soothing hand it is which wipeth the tears that scald and blister where they fall; thy melting touch it is which biddeth them to flow when the sudden shock of dread calamity denies the sufferer the relief they bring to the stricken heart; without thee the world were a barren and dry land, and the heavens were as brass above us; but, lo! we see thee now in the full glory of thy beauty as thou standest revealed to us in the tears of Jesus.

Nine-tenths of the so-called friendships of the world are make-believes. The links of fellowship hold together only so long as there is no strain upon them; at the first touch of trial they snap asunder. So long as the association is agreeable or flattering to either party, or serves some kind of purpose, it is all well; but at the first call for the exercise of self-denial, self-sacrifice, where is your friend? You are under a cloud, perhaps. Misfortune has fallen upon you—maybe the ban of undeserved suspicion. You rush to your friend for advice and comfort, and find that he is not at home. Thenceforward, until you have cleared yourself, and the cloud has passed away, he is never at home to you. But should the sun of prosperity shine upon you again, how sorry he will be for your past troubles; how delighted he will be to call upon you and offer his congratulations. Away with such fair-weather friends! Such cannot hope to gain the friendship of Christ, who bestowed words of consolation upon the Magdalene, and wept at the grave of Lazarus tears of such evident heartfelt sympathy that those around Him were convinced beyond doubt how He must have loved him. What a testimony was this to the friendship of the Bethany household for Christ, that He accepted it and reciprocated it! Lazarus must surely have been a good and pure-hearted man so to have won the heart of Jesus. It was a great thing to be said of any man that our Lord took pleasure in his society; a happy thing to be said of him that he delighted in the companionship of our Lord. Now and again at Bethany, in the cool of the evening, Jesus and Lazarus might doubtless have been seen walking under the olive trees, engaged in loving converse. The eye of the traveller as he passed would only see two young men, who had evidently their tastes and pursuits in common, and had struck up a very natural friendship together; but God and the angels saw there a far more wondrous and more beauteous sight—the beloved Son, in whom the Father was well pleased, consoled in His earthly pilgrimage to the Cross with the tender and reverent regard of a good and upright man.

Brother, sister, value your friendships when they are formed upon the solid foundations of loving sincerity and sterling goodness; choose your friends carefully—aye, prayerfully, and when you have got them, keep them. Whatever may separate you, be not yourself the cause. Prepare for any measure of self-sacrifice (do not sacrifice *others* to your friends), be ready at any moment to do a real service, and you will not regret it hereafter, whatever may be your loss in this world. For the culture of true friendship is a means of education for the society of heaven, and for the companionship of the pure and loving Jesus, which is the greatest bliss of the saints in light. No faithless soul will be admitted to the company of those blessed ones who have been found worthy of the friendship of Jesus Christ. No one who will not deny himself for his friend's sake need hope for the favour and blessing of God upon his friendship. "Greater love," said our great Exemplar, "hath no man than this, that a man lay down his life for his friends." And though men are rarely called upon to perform this highest act of self-devotion, still it is essential to the perfect development of our friendships that we lay down for them something that we hold dear. Sacrifice of self is the glory of true affection.

Then, in addition to those friends we choose for ourselves, there are those who are bestowed upon us by the good providence of God. I mean our home friends. The same principle of self-sacrifice applies with even greater force in the home; for it is the home-life that makes continual demands upon us, the yielding of our own will in little things from day to day. Now we all know there are many households in which the ties of kindred, although of the closest, do not include real friendship. These human souls dwell together year after year, have many interests and pursuits in common, fight bravely for each other's claims as against strangers, and yet probably are far from being truly friends. "Oh, it is only my brother," or "only my sister," or "it's only mother," is a phrase too often heard upon the lips of such as these—as though the fact of close relationship were a sufficient excuse for want of proper consideration, for neglect of the ordinary and necessary courtesies of life. "Woman, behold thy son!" Ah, what tender solicitude is here! We may be sure that from first to last of our Lord's earthly life He paid His mother the same loving respect as when He hung upon the cross. The sword that pierced her anguished soul was none of His handling; we may rest assured that those sayings of His which she lovingly kept and pondered in her heart from His childhood upwards, had nothing in them to wound her love. I have known more than one graceless young fellow who seemed to reserve all his good-humour for his out-of-door companions, and to expend all his ill-temper upon his home and his mother—his mother in chief, because she was so long-suffering, and bore it all so bravely for the great love which she had for her son. We cannot say much for the manliness of sons like these. They are not of the stuff that heroes are made of; beware of choosing such an one for your friend. For every true friend is a hero in heart, ready to do and to suffer for those whom he loves.

Lastly, there is no limit to the duration of true friendships on both sides—not even death. Did Jesus cease to be the Friend of Lazarus when He ascended to the Father? Nay, He went thither to prepare a place for His beloved friend. Did Lazarus cease to be the friend of Jesus when, a second time, he died? Nay, for that best part of him, his immortal spirit, went to the Paradise prepared by Jesus, where he lives in joy and peace, rejoicing in the fellowship of his dear Lord and Elder Brother—a fellowship to be made most perfect, most complete, in the Day of the Resurrection of the Body. And such eternal human fellowship may be ours also, with our earthly friends; but most of all, with the Man Christ Jesus. Yes, my brethren, the same perfect human love, the same exalting fellowship that He bestowed on Lazarus, and on St. John, may be yours if you strive for it. Is it not worth striving for? You cannot be sure of the continuance of any friendship of this world, however strong, however dear. Death is the only seal which, when it is set upon a friendship, makes it secure for ever. And that brings with it the agony of parting in the flesh. But the friendship of Jesus is the strongest and the surest; there is no pain of parting from Him; for the hour of death is the hour of the Lord's tryst with you, that you may see Him face to face, and in that glad moment realise far more than in this life is possible to you, what it is to have Jesus for your Friend. Behold, how He loves you.

V.

"Behold, a Voice."

Like a single bright star, for one moment out shining,
Then hidden for mists all the firmament lining,
    That vision was given;
But the light of that Cloud still their souls overshading,
And the sound of that Voice from their hearts never fading,
    Was their beacon to heaven.

C. L. Ford.

V.

"Behold, a Voice."

(ST. MATT. xvii. 5.)

FROM the beginning of miracles in Cana of Galilee, Christ manifested forth His glory in numberless ways before the world, even before those bitter enemies of His who were ever on the alert to "catch" Him; but the special manifestation of His glory, the glory made visible in His own Person, was reserved for the chosen three—St. Peter, St. James, and St. John. Why only these three disciples were permitted to look upon the revealing wonder of the Transfiguration we are not told; but we may perhaps endeavour to understand why, by a rough kind of analogy drawn from the phenomena of every-day life.

You may meet a man from day to day in the ordinary course of business, or in your journeyings to and from your own house; and these encounters, voluntary or accidental, may go on for years until your idea of that person has unconsciously become stereotyped in your mind, as that of a matter-of-fact, business-hardened individual. At last it may happen that your intercourse takes a more personal, a more intimate turn, and you are asked one day to accompany him to his home. Once the threshold is passed and the door is closed upon the outer world, and the welcoming smiles of the wife and the happy voices of the children greet the husband and father, a subtle change passes over him : the hard lines round the mouth and over the brows relax as by magic, and the face of that man is transfigured before you. And why? Because he is at home—because he is in an atmosphere where all that is best and truest in his nature spontaneously manifests itself, evoked by the love of his nearest and dearest. The true self of the man shines forth in his face, for he has regained his earthly sanctuary, he has re-entered upon the happiness, the relief, the rest, of home.

The same kind of manifestation is familiar to

us in many other minor forms. For instance, you may enter into conversation with some new acquaintance who for a time may appear to be utterly devoid of individuality—or at any rate of responsiveness. You try one topic after another, only to meet with common-place replies or irrelevant observations. At last, as though by accident, you make some allusion to a subject which takes instant effect upon your companion. His face brightens up, his eyes flash with excitement, and almost before you are aware of the change, the tongue which a moment before was so cold and hesitating, is now eloquent upon the darling theme of that man's heart. For the time his whole being is transformed by the enthusiasm which expands and irradiates it; and your startled conviction proclaims as with a voice of power that the man before you is entitled to be heard, for with that one subject, if with no other in the world, he is thoroughly and entirely at home.

I have known more than one musician of great genius whose ordinary expression and appearance seemed lacking in either animation or refinement; whom, indeed, if you met him in a crowd, you might take to be a man of very ordinary tastes and pursuits; but see him as he listens to the music of some great master, to the language of some kindred spirit; and the wondrous illumination which plays over his countenance—the flashing eye, the quivering lip, and the thoughtful brow, all is as speaking as though an audible voice were heard to say, "Here, indeed, is a true-born son of his immortal art."

But oh, how imperfect, how infinitely inferior are these phenomena of our human life, when we are brought within view of that most ineffable glory—the Transfiguration of the Man of Sorrows! Those poor instances of mine I should hardly have dared to name as analogies, but for this one thing which they have in common—that whereas the visible glory of the Transfiguration as seen in Jesus is impossible to sinful man, because light cannot shine forth out of our darkness; it was after all only natural to Him, because it was inherent in Him who is the Light of the World —in whom was no darkness of sin.

But I said at the outset that we might perhaps gain some kind of idea why this special manifestation of Christ's glory was confined to the three favoured disciples. Their stronger faith and love had proved them more worthy than the rest of being taken into His confidence, and of being admitted to a glimpse of the inner sanctuary of their Master's spiritual life, to the privilege of being near to Him while He was verily at home with His Father, and with the indwellers of His Father's House. It was while in the happy communion, the spiritual relief and rest of prayer, that the fashion of His countenance was altered; it was the inward rapture of love and devotion which burgeoned into the glistering whiteness of His outward form; and this revealing of His inmost self, His spiritual being, was no sight for a curious and gaping crowd. It was no premeditated formal demonstration of supernatural splendour designed to overawe the unbelief of a reluctant world. Rather was it a faithful representation, a living exemplification, of the glorious destiny of the perfect Man—that is, of man made perfect before God in the righteousness of Jesus Christ.

And, further, we begin to see why, when the manifestation had passed, our blessed Saviour so strictly charged those three whom He had taken into His confidence that they should tell no man what they had just seen, and to keep His secret until He had risen from the dead. It was good for them to be there and to see His glory; but had they spread abroad the things they had witnessed, the multitude, ever eager—then as now—for some new phenomenon or sign, would have followed Him up the mountain height to pry into the presence chamber of His communion with the Father. This could not be permitted; for just as home is home no longer when its sacred privacy is subject to the constant intrusion of strangers, so is the solitude of the mountain top no longer a sanctuary, no longer a meeting-place with God, when it is broken in upon by profane or careless spectators. And so Jesus charged them to tell no man of the wondrous scene they had witnessed of that human face and form thus glorified in virtue of perfect fellowship with the Father and of the Communion of Saints. But the great lesson, for them and for us, of this manifestation came from the mouth of the eternal Father Himself out of the bright cloud, the Shekinah of His presence that enwrapt them; for behold, a Voice out of the cloud which said—" This is My Beloved Son in whom I am well pleased : Hear ye Him!"

It is a trite enough saying, my brethren, that the world is full of voices. The poet, the artist, the philosopher, the man of science, each hears speaking to him voices which are inaudible or inarticulate to the other, as well as to the rest of the world—and this because these other natures are lacking in that special faculty, of whatever order, which receives and understands the communications that move the impulses and fructify the conceptions of the realm of art, or philosophy, or science. But there is one Voice which all the world may hear, and does hear, in varying degrees of distinctness; in the ears of the many it is only a far-away inarticulate murmur, of which they become faintly conscious in the fitful pauses of life; while on the ears of some it falls ever and anon with startling tones of condemnation, or, rarer still, with gentle accents of loving approval. It is the same Voice that spoke in the garden—"Adam, where art thou?"—the same Voice that spake from the dark cloud in thunders upon Sinai; that proclaimed the beloved Son at the baptism in Jordan, and again from the bright cloud on the Mount of Transfiguration. And of these two proclamations of the Divine approval of the Son of Man, only the Baptist heard the first, only the three disciples heard the second. I say advisedly the Divine approval of the Son of Man, for although He was verily, and in no mere figurative sense, the eternal Son of God, the Only-begotten of the Father, was it not as Man that He was baptised with the Baptism of John—as Man that he spake with Moses and Elias of the decease which He was shortly to accomplish at Jerusalem? Let us not lose grasp of this great and all-inspiring fact; let us cling gratefully and adoringly to the Hand of that perfect humanity which brings us so close to God ; which leads us into the presence chamber of the Most High, and to the blest society of just men made perfect, as to a Home of peace and joy, and love and rest, which even on earth we can be allowed to enter in the name of our transfigured Lord. For although the glory and the voice were seen and heard by those only who bare record, that record has become the inheritance of mankind ; in heart and spirit and with reverent devotion we may witness with them the manifestation of the unity of man with God through the perfect Manhood of Jesus Christ our Lord ; and share with them the demonstration of His acceptance with the Father, by the living Voice which bids us hear Him. " He that hath ears to hear, let him hear."

Behold, a Voice. Yes, my brothers, there is a Voice which speaks to every man, upon every act of his life, recording the unerring judgment of the eternal Father. Call it conscience, or by any other name you will, it is the Voice of God alone that speaks in authoritative approval or condemnation. We may stop our ears, but we cannot stop the Voice from speaking. We are conscious that our thoughts, our words, our deeds are such as to merit no word of Divine approval, however loudly they may be applauded by the voice of man; we stop our ears, for we dread to hear the voice of judgment; we try to rush away from the sound of it; we try to drown it in the hubbub of the world's excitements; we try to ignore it altogether; but strive against it as we may, there are moments of solitude and silence when in spite of ourselves we must listen, and own in trembling that the sentence is a just sentence.

Many a life has been ruined, both for this world and the next, by the perversity which has refused to listen to that Voice. Many a young man, setting out full of hope upon his chosen career, fresh from the salutary restraints and the tender solicitude of home, with a father's blessing and a mother's prayers attending him from the threshold, has found that Voice sounding in his ears with solemn warning at the first suggestions of temptation. He knows full well, for he has been carefully taught that lesson from childhood upwards, that the only path of safety is the path of duty and self-denial, that the only sanctuary of sure refuge from evil is to be gained in the mountain fastness of prayer and communion with God, that if he would hope to hear the "Well done" of the great Master of Life, he must stedfastly and with all his might press forward in the steps of the Saviour. And if he remain true to the training of his early years, if he continue to walk worthy of the vocation wherewith he was called in his baptism, the Voice shall one day greet him with the words of Divine approval, and he shall in his own turn be proclaimed and acknowledged before his brethren—before the two or three that know him best—as a beloved son of God by adoption and grace. But, alas! how rare a consummation is this. How often the first allurements of the Tempter beguile the young man into the bye-paths of lawless pleasures and debasing pursuits and ambitions! There comes a time when he forsakes the path of the upward life which leads to the heaven-touching peaks of the soul's transfiguration, and he finds too late the downward track of guilt and shame hurrying him on with ever-increasing impetus into the abyss of eternal ruin.

At this moment there rises before me a picture of startling vividness, the fearful ending of one such young man. Nurtured with the fondest care, endowed with rare qualities of mind and heart, the favoured one amongst his compeers, with a grand career before him—and yet, almost at the very outset of a life so full of hope and promise, I see him stretched upon a miserable pallet in a yet more miserable garret, with "that across his throat" one may well shudder to look upon, and his face, once so handsome and so bright that every one felt the happier for seeing it, now cold and ashen, and the glazed eyeballs staring grim and ghastly in the grey pallor of the dawn.

But I am speaking rather to those whose ears are open, or may yet be opened, to the Voice of God, as it comes to us in the still small voice of conscience, whispering to us in the midst of life's noisy conflict, or, perchance, in the wakeful watches of the night. Rarely, if ever, does it speak save in solemn warning and reproof, for it is generally in the act of sin, or in the memory of a sin, that we hear the Voice saying, as it did to the first man who sinned, "Adam, where art thou?" And if that question drive us to shame, so that we would fain hide ourselves from the presence of God, it is only natural to our fallen condition; but let us not imitate the action of Adam further than this. Let us not take false refuge in miserable subterfuge, in shifty excuses for the palliation of our guilt. Adam's clumsy and cowardly attempt at defence was of no avail with God. Nor, for all we may imagine or Satan suggest as to mitigating circumstances, have we any better defence to offer. Nay, let us down with our false pride, let us humble ourselves before our Father against whom we have sinned, and own with contrition the blackness of our sinful hearts. And then He whose perfect righteousness was typified—nay, rather exhibited—in the glory of the Transfiguration will take us by the hand, and we, standing with Him thus before

God, shall hear the voice of love and forgiveness breathing peace and consolation into our hearts. Yes, we have an Intercessor, an High Priest touched with the feeling of our infirmities; for the Beloved Son in whom God is well pleased is none other than the Man of Sorrows, the Man who is acquainted with our grief.

There is one aspect of the Transfiguration on which I have casually touched; but it is far too precious a truth to be hastily brushed by. It is, that by this act our blessed Lord prefigured the true destiny of humanity. Now, we often speak of Him as raising our human nature, as elevating us to the dignity of sons of God; but with too many of us these are little more than figures of speech. My brethren, Christ did not die to supply us with figures of speech. He did not live among us to give us ideas, but an ideal. And that ideal was no tantalising impossibility, for with the help of God all things are made possible. And so, when by taking our nature upon Him, Christ purified and transfigured it, He proved to us how, by divine assistance, our manhood could be purified and transfigured. Why need He have encumbered Himself with our mortal frame for thirty years and more but for that high and most gracious purpose? Why need the Only Begotten have left the bosom of the Father to enter into the actual experience of every petty detail of man's life unless it was to demonstrate that every such detail of human existence could be made glorious by the power which He had in Himself and was able to impart to every man? You will tell me that He did all this to assure us of His practical sympathy in all our little trials and difficulties, and that is quite true; but it was for more than this. He taught us how we might rise superior to them, not by shirking them, or rebelling against the discipline they brought us, but by looking beyond them to the magnificent destiny for which God created us, the heritage of immortal sonship. In His own Divine yet human Person he demonstrated the compatibility of a glorified and everlasting manhood with the frail earthly elements of a body unto which it is appointed once to die. He taught us how, by the virtue of that immortal essence impregnating those frail elements, our sinful bodies may be made like unto His body, and, therefore, capable at the resurrection of the same wondrous transfiguration which glorified His human Body on the Mount. And, more than all, He taught us how we may prefigure in our present existence that resurrection change, by conforming ourselves to the conditions of a consecrated life, a will brought into harmony with the will of God, a heart joined in communion by prayer and by service with the great heart of the all-loving Father — essential conditions, from which must follow, as light succeeds darkness, the transfiguration of the inward man, the renewal of his likeness in the image of God.

And how shall we hope to attain to this dignity of ours? Once more let us listen to the voice out of the cloud: "This is my beloved Son, *hear ye Him.*" Yes, for to hear Him is to draw nigh to Him; to draw nigh should surely be to receive Him into our hearts; and as many as receive Him to them giveth He power to become the sons of God. And how does He impart to us that wondrous power? Is it not by the indwelling and the moving and the leading of the Holy Spirit of God? For as many as are led by the Spirit of God, they are the sons of God. And so the voice of the Spirit shall be heard in sweet assurance of the greatness of our destiny, He Himself bearing witness with our spirit that we are children of God; and if children, then heirs, heirs of God and joint-heirs with Christ, if so be that we suffer with Him, that we may also be glorified with Him.*

Take, then, this Charter Deed, my brothers in Christ, this patent of a dignity which is veritably yours; take it and compare it, contrast it with the most splendid-sounding scheme ever devised by the intellect of man for the exaltation of the human race, and you will see for yourselves how miserably empty and vague are the promises and the prophesyings of those who would lure us away from the definite and tangible realities of our holy religion. Tell the trans-

* Cf. Rom. viii. 16, 17, Revised Version.

cendentalist that the spiritual mysteries of the Kingdom of God are immeasurably above and beyond his fondest dreams; tell the Positivist that Christ enriches and ennobles your present life with the practical benefits of a daily contact with His real humanity; tell the whole world, the struggling, fighting, fainting, dying humanity around you, that all may share with you that eternal inheritance, that most majestic sonship, which is the unfailing portion of all in whose lives are reflected the transfiguration glories of the Man of Sorrows.

VI.

"Behold, the Lamb of God!"

BEHOLD HIM, ALL YE PASSERS BY,
   THE LAMB OF GOD, THE LIFE DIVINE!
COME, SINNERS, SEE YOUR MAKER DIE;
   HE CRIES, WAS EVER GRIEF LIKE MINE?
THE LORD OF LIFE FOR ALL HAS DIED,
   OUR LORD, OUR LOVE, IS CRUCIFIED.

J. Wesley.

VI.

"Behold, the Lamb of God!"

(ST. JOHN i. 36.)

THIS exclamation of the Baptist must have astonished those who heard it. For it pointed out Jesus as a Victim, as a Sacrifice, as One to be offered up.

The Baptist's expression, "Lamb of God," had but one meaning to the Jews. God's Lamb was the Lamb of Sacrifice, pure, harmless, perfect, without spot or blemish. And in every one of these respects we are taught to look upon the Divine Jesus as God's Lamb, bearing, and so taking away, the sins of the world.

And here, my brethren, on the very threshold of this great subject, we are brought into contact with a mystery, a Divine mystery which we cannot, being mortal, apprehend except by the eye of faith. Our puny human intellect can only ask in wonderment the how and the why, and obtain no answer of explanation. Little children often ask us concerning the smaller mysteries of our present life, and we cannot answer them, well as we may understand many of them ourselves, because we feel that the little ones can only grow up into the knowledge of them. They must pass from childhood to manhood, in order that natural development or individual experience may reveal what no arguments or explanations of ours can bring home to them. Our reply to their "how" and their "why" is, wait until you have grown up into man's estate, and you will understand it all well enough then. And as it is between the children and ourselves, so is it between ourselves and God. In the presence of the great mysteries of our faith God says to us, wait until you have grown up into that higher estate in comparison with which you are now but babes. Yet a little while and the veil shall be removed, and ye who wait in humble faith shall see Me face to face and know all these things.

But very few children are satisfied with their elders' advice to them to wait. Not only is the counsel unpalatable because it makes demands on their faith and patience, but they cannot conceive their own inability to understand our explanations. But how strange it is that we, men and women, having in familiar phrase "grown up," and now seeing the full force of our parents' advice to wait, nevertheless go on imagining that our minds can comprehend those mysteries which our Heavenly Father tells us we cannot grasp in our present imperfect and immature spiritual estate! In His ineffable condescension He has told us all, explained to us all, that we can possibly understand in this life; and for what is beyond us He asks our faith and patience, not as awaiting His good pleasure to reveal it or withhold it —though such should ever be our attitude towards Him—but that in the process of our spiritual development, which can only reach maturity on the other side of the grave, we may gradually grow into the knowledge of all that wondrous plan which the very angels desired to look into.

We are nowhere told that St. John Baptist was able to comprehend the height and depth of the mystery of the Great Sacrifice when he exclaimed, "Behold, the Lamb of God!" This acknowledgment was the result of a native intuition, illuminated and expanded by the Spirit of the Lord which was upon him as the prophet—yea, more than a prophet—whose mission it was to prepare the way of the Lord. I say a native intuition, because he must have felt as a man, and still more as a Jew, that the great and all-availing Sacrifice had yet to be offered; and the Spirit within him, whose Voice he was to that generation, taught him to recognise in the Person of the Divine Jesus, that Lamb of Sacrifice. For the Baptist, being but man, and like his great prototype Elijah, subject to like passions and therefore to like infirmities with ourselves, was not able to penetrate within the shrine of the awful mysteries which he proclaimed; he could only receive them, as we can and must receive them, by the operation of faith, assisted by the blessed Spirit of God.

What then did the Baptist himself understand, and what did he intend to convey, in this acknowledgment and proclamation of Jesus as the Lamb of God? Nothing more, nothing less, than the Church of Christ understands and proclaims to-day. He saw prospectively, as we see realised, the redemption of the world by the sacrifice of the Lamb of God, and he recognised and identified that very Paschal Lamb in the Person of Jesus Christ. He saw united in that one Person the essential elements of the perfect Sacrifice, the Divine nature of the Only-begotten Son of God with the human nature of the son of Adam,—without sin as the Spotless Lamb must be, but yet capable of the suffering and humiliation that pertains to frail humanity—at once the all-sufficient and the only possible Mediator and Redeemer. But when we say "the only possible," we must qualify the term as Hooker correspondingly qualifies the term "impossible" in his well-known passage on this subject. "The world's salvation," he says, "was without the Incarnation of the Son of God impossible, not simply impossible, but impossible, it being presupposed that the will of God was no otherwise to have it saved than by the death of His own Son. Therefore taking to Himself our flesh; and by His Incarnation making it His own flesh, He had none of His own, although from us, what to offer unto God for us."* In his last words we catch a partial glimpse of the matchless perfectness and grace of God's plan of salvation—that is, as far as the giant intellect of Hooker spiritualised by close communion with God was able to compass—but more than this we may not in this life hope to see. Our souls can dwell, and by dwelling grow and fructify in the light of this great fact, but we may not, we cannot separate the constituent rays of that spiritual glory in any poor

* "Eccles. Polity," Bk. v. 51.

spectrum of our own devising. And what need to analyse it, when our souls can feel the warmth of the Divine Love which is at the heart of the mystery?

Let us behold, then, in God's Lamb, the Embodiment of the love of God to the world. Ever since the world began our Creator had assured us of His compassion and mercy: in His dealings with nations and with individuals He had manifested His providential care; in His more intimate connection with the Chosen People He had shown Himself a God of marvellous long-suffering and loving-kindness; but all these older manifestations of Divine Love were now summed and perfected in that one crowning act, the gift of His Only-begotten Son to be the Lamb slain for the sins of the world. It was as though our Heavenly Father were so bent on convincing us of the reality, the immensity of His love towards us, that He must needs prove it in that form in which our own natures could but appreciate it, however imperfectly. For an earthly parent to give up his own and only son in an unselfish cause is rightly considered the greatest gift he can bestow; and so to win our love and gratitude as well as to procure our redemption, "God spared not His Only-begotten Son, but freely gave Him up for us all."

Who can withstand the overwhelming evidence of love like this? It is above the unaided conception of the human mind to associate such tender love and mercy with the idea of an Almighty Ruler of the universe, a Sovereign Arbiter of mortal destinies. The omnipotent deity of the heathen is a cruel and heartless monster desiring to annihilate rather than to save mankind. The heathen poet* tells us how the agonizing tortures of an immortal were due to the jealous anger of Jupiter at his having befriended and assisted the human race. What a contrast is this to the revelation we have of the God of Heaven and earth! The god of the heathen is furious with one who saves mortals from Hades; the God whom we love

---

* Æschylus, "Prom. Vinct.," 231 *sqq.*

and adore gives up His only Son that all men might be saved.

And yet, even in the presence of this wondrous revelation, how persistent are the opponents of our faith in their misrepresentations of the Divine wisdom and love. One of them—a leading spirit among them—has recently shown how grossly the doctrine of God's great manifestation of love to mankind can be perverted, when he speaks of it as "effecting a reconciliation by sacrificing a son who was perfectly innocent, to satisfy the assumed necessity for a propitiatory victim."* It surely needs no subtleness of intellect to seize upon the miserable fallacies which vainly try to hide in these specious words. For the idea which they seek to foist upon us is that of the heathen, that of a god as inconsistent in his motives and actions as he is relentless and tyrannical, guilty of a needless act of cruelty for the mere gratification of a whim. They assume that the Son of God was an involuntary, helpless sacrifice.

* *Nineteenth Century*, No. 83, p. 6.

They assume that mankind had no need of redemption or reconciliation. And in all this they assume in those they address an overwhelming ignorance of the Word of God, which on these essential matters is so plain that a child may understand it. For we know that the Lamb that was slain was none other than God Himself in the Person of His Son; we know that the Son's sacrifice was a willing sacrifice, not that of a shrinking terrified victim. We know that the need of a God-appointed means of reconciliation is a felt need; a need whose range is too universal for argument, whose root is too deep for doubting.

And so, rising above the heart-aching controversies which in the ears of God must sound like so many petty disputes of children, let us look upon the glories of the Lamb that was slain, and in the only attitude that will repay us. We shall find that the best glimpse of that most Divine glory is only to be got by kneeling. For the sense of our own unworthiness must surely bring us to our knees. There are times —as we have already seen—times in every man's life when the Voice within him is heard to pronounce sentence of condemnation against him, and he is fain to exclaim with Job, "Behold, I am vile." If he be content after that self-revelation to let the stain remain upon his soul, and deepen there past eradication, no system of philosophy will pretend to justify him. But if, on the other hand, he cannot endure the thought of that hideous blot upon his life's record, he will desire to remove it if possible by repentance and reparation. But he will find that reparation is not in every case possible; he will find that the greater the sin the less able he is to atone for it. He will, of course, resolve to amend his ways, but he feels that this resolution even if carried into effect will not wipe out the sin of the past, that regret and remorse for having committed that sin will not cancel it. He feels —I am assuming that a man is honest with himself—that he cannot pronounce his own absolution, that the taking away of that fearful burden must come from a source external to himself. To whom is he to turn—to his fellow-men—his fellow-sinners? No man can be supposed able to forgive him for the injury he has inflicted upon his own soul. Can he recognise his brethren in the mass as a kind of deity (as some in the present day are unconsciously endeavouring to do), and cry out, "O Humanity, forgive my sins, and restore peace to my soul!" His best instincts revolt against such a preposterous sham. They tell him that only a higher power than humanity can relieve him of the burden of his sins: that they must be atoned for by some one who has no sin of his own to atone for; by one who has both the will and ability to atone, and the authority and will to pardon: and his sense of need impels him to cry out for that One, to abase himself before that One, and as he falls upon his knees under the weight of his sin and the pressure of his necessity, behold, there comes to him the revelation of the Lamb of God, bearing and taking away his sins, with all the sins of the world.

But how, you will ask, are we to see in all this the glories of the Man of Sorrows? Are you not pointing us rather to the glory of God? Yes, truly this is one of the glories of the Most Highest, but only as revealed to us in the Person of the Man Christ Jesus. Weakness and subjection, pain and conflict, cannot be ascribed to the Godhead—we may not speak of a God of Sorrows. But the eternal Word, the Creator of the world, of His own will became man, once and for always:—took upon Him the form and the nature of one of His own creatures, in order that He might supply in His own Person that need of a Saviour which is inherent in sinful man. In Jesus Christ we are taught to distinguish the two natures of Divine and human—to distinguish them, but we cannot separate them, and therefore we see in the glory of Jesus as perfect Man, the glory of Christ as God.

Here, then, is the wondrous paradox to which I referred at the outset of these meditations—the Omnipotent God tabernacling in a weak and suffering man; the Omniscient God dwelling in a child that grew in wisdom as in stature.

in the natural course and order of human development; the Sovereign God enshrined in the form of a servant, who became obedient unto death, even the death of the Cross. And as we contemplate this dread mystery, we feel that no man or body of men could have conceived it, or even if they had conceived it, have dared of their own motion and authority to place such a paradox before the world. But the world has had experience of the power and operation of that mystery upon the hearts and lives of men, by the miracles which its presence amongst us has wrought continually for eighteen hundred years. "Lo, I am with you alway, even unto the end of the world."

And so in the Lamb of God we see the glory of voluntary and sinless suffering for the sins of men. We see it most clearly of all when we kneel at the foot of the Cross, bowed down by the sense of our sins, and when turning to the Crucified with our confession of shame we behold at once the atonement made, the absolution given. All sin is there atoned for; no one need rise from thence unpardoned. Not only was God's Lamb a willing sacrifice, but a perfect sacrifice. What a glorious assurance for sinners in every kind and degree! To harbour for a moment the thought that there is a single sin of yours unatoned for is to rob your Saviour of the honour and glory due unto His name. The Lamb that was slain is God's Lamb; the God you have sinned against appointed and accepted that sacrifice as all-sufficient,—sufficient for you and for me.

> "Then once more pray:
> Down with thy knees, up with thy voice:
> Seek pardon first, and God will say—
> *Glad heart rejoyce.*" *

But while you rejoice, rejoice with weeping. For never forget in the joy of deliverance that it was your sin which caused the suffering and the death of Jesus. For if man—that is, you and I, had not sinned, there had been no need of atonement for sin. The keenest sorrows of the Saviour were not His bodily sufferings—

* George Herbert.

these were as nothing in comparison with His grief for the sin that defiled His beautiful creation, that had debased and ruined His last, best work, man made in His own image. Behold and see if there was any sorrow like unto that sorrow of His. Let us aspire to the blessed privilege of sharing in this chief sorrow of Jesus, His sorrow for sin. St. Paul counted it a signal honour to bear in his own body the marks of his Lord, to share in some sort His stripes and afflictions, to wear the thorny crown of fellowship in His sufferings. It is unlikely that any of us will be called upon to take the share in them that St. Paul had, small as that was when compared with the colossal Passion of the Garden and the Cross. But the more we contemplate the Passion, the better shall we be enabled to enter into sympathy with the Sufferer, to look at sin as it were with His eyes, and therefore in some feeble measure to feel the pain of it in our own souls. Yes, in this way let us strive to suffer with Jesus. For it is only by sharing His sufferings that we can be permitted to share His glory. It is a condition of our kinship, our coheirship with Christ. We must suffer with Him, St. Paul reminds us, in order that we may be glorified with Him.

Behold, the Lamb of God. Think, then, what this means for you and me. It means that when the Voice cries to us Behold, we are not merely to gaze as bystanders, but to fix our eyes upon the Sacrifice appointed for us, following God's Lamb all along the rugged way that leads through Gethsemane to the hill of Calvary. It means that we are to plead that Sacrifice, each one for himself, before the throne of God. It means that we are to plead it in contrition and self-abasement, if we would obtain remission of our sins. It means, further, that looking upon the sorrows of Jesus we shall learn how to suffer with Him, that is, to feel the pain and the wickedness and misery of sin. And above all, it means that having learned to suffer with the Man of Sorrows, we shall share His glory in this life and in the life to come. In this life? Aye, my brothers, His glory shall be in you and shine out of you by the power of His Spirit in your hearts. For even as on earth He manifested forth His glory in His own life and acts; so now on earth He still manifests His glory by the life and acts of every true disciple: and amid all the trials and conflicts of this life,—and some of them, God knows, are heavy enough to bear—the abiding happiness of a soul in union with God will be yours, illuminating not only your inmost being but your external life, and thus bearing witness before men that you have been with Jesus,—that He, the Lamb of God who taketh away the sins of the world, hath taken away your sins and granted you His peace. And thus living, and so dying in that peace, you shall hereafter behold, and beholding receive in yourselves in an infinitely higher degree that glory of the Lamb which St. John the Divine saw in the heavenly vision of the Revelation, when you, joining your voice with the voices of the ten thousand times ten thousand, shall give praise to the Lamb that was slain.

The Old Testament Commentary for English Readers.

Edited by the RIGHT REV. C. J. ELLICOTT, D.D.,
Lord Bishop of Gloucester and Bristol.

COMPLETE IN FIVE VOLUMES.

VOLUME I., *price 21s., contains—*

PREFACE	By the Lord Bishop of GLOUCESTER and BRISTOL.
GENERAL INTRODUCTION	By the Very Rev. Dean PLUMPTRE, D.D.
GENESIS	By the Very Rev. Dean PAYNE SMITH, D.D.
EXODUS	By the Rev. Canon RAWLINSON, M.A.
LEVITICUS	By the Rev. C. D. GINSBURG, LL.D., Author of "The Massorah."
NUMBERS	By the late Rev. Canon ELLIOTT, M.A.

VOLUME II., *price 21s., contains—*

DEUTERONOMY AND JOSHUA	By the Rev. C. H. WALLER, M.A.
JUDGES	By the Ven. Archdeacon FARRAR, D.D., F.R.S.
RUTH	By the Rev. R. SINKER, B.D.
I. SAMUEL	By the Rev. Canon SPENCE, M.A.
II. SAMUEL	By the Rev. Prof. GARDINER, D.D.

VOLUME III., *price 21s., contains—*

I. KINGS	By the Right Rev. ALFRED BARRY, D.D., Bishop of Sydney and Primate of Australia.
II. KINGS	By the Rev. C. J. BALL, M.A.
I. AND II CHRONICLES	
EZRA	By the Rev. W. B. POPE, D.D.
NEHEMIAH	
ESTHER	By the Rev. R. SINKER, B.D.

VOLUME IV., *price 21s., contains—*

JOB	By the Rev. Prof. STANLEY LEATHES, D.D.
PSALMS	By the Rev. A. S. AGLEN, M.A.
PROVERBS	By the Rev. J. W. NUTT, M.A., late Fellow of All Souls, Oxford.
ECCLESIASTES	By the Rev. Prof. SALMON, D.D., College, Dublin.
SONG OF SOLOMON	By the Rev. A. S. AGLEN, M.A.
ISAIAH	By the Very Rev. Dean PLUMPTRE, D.D.

VOLUME V., *price 21s., contains—*

JEREMIAH	By the Very Rev. Dean PLUMPTRE, D.D.
LAMENTATIONS	
EZEKIEL	By the Rev. F. GARDINER, D.D.
DANIEL	By the Rev. HENRY DEANE, B.D.
HOSEA	By the Rev. H. R. REYNOLDS and the Rev. Prof. WHITEHOUSE.
JOEL	By the Rev. S. L. WARREN, M.A.
AMOS	By the Rev. H. R. REYNOLDS, D.D., and the Rev. Prof. WHITEHOUSE.
OBADIAH	By the Rev. A. S. AGLEN, M.A.
JONAH	
MICAH	By the Rev. S. L. WARREN.
NAHUM, HABAKKUK, ZEPHANIAH, AND HAGGAI	By the Rev. A. C. JENNINGS, M.A.
ZECHARIAH	By the Rev. W. H. LOWE, M.A.
MALACHI	

CASSELL & COMPANY. LIMITED, *London; and all Booksellers.*

The New Testament Commentary
for English Readers.

Edited by the RIGHT REV. C. J. ELLICOTT, D.D.,
Lord Bishop of Gloucester and Bristol.

Complete in Three Vols., price 21s. each, or bound in half-morocco, £4 14s. 6d. the set.

VOLUME I., *price 21s., contains—*

ST. MATTHEW	⎫
ST. MARK	⎬ By Very Rev. Dean PLUMPTRE, D.D.
ST. LUKE	⎭
ST. JOHN	By Ven. Archdeacon WATKINS, D.D.

VOLUME II., *price 21s., contains—*

THE ACTS OF THE APOSTLES	By Very Rev. Dean PLUMPTRE, D.D.
ROMANS	By Rev. W. SANDAY, M.A., D.D.
CORINTHIANS I.	By Rev. T. TEIGNMOUTH SHORE, M.A.
CORINTHIANS II.	By Very Rev. Dean PLUMPTRE, D.D.
GALATIANS	By Rev. W. SANDAY, M.A., D.D.

VOLUME III., *price 21s., contains—*

EPHESIANS	⎫ By Right Rev. ALFRED BARRY, D.D.,
PHILIPPIANS	⎬ Bishop of Sydney and Primate of Australia.
COLOSSIANS	⎭
THESSALONIANS I. and II.	By Rev. Canon MASON, M.A.
TIMOTHY I. and II.	⎫ By Rev. Canon SPENCE, M.A.
TITUS	⎭
PHILEMON	By Right Rev. ALFRED BARRY, D.D.
HEBREWS	By Rev. W. F. MOULTON, D.D.
ST. JAMES	By Rev. E. G. PUNCHARD, M.A.
ST. PETER I.	By Rev. Canon MASON, M.A.
ST. PETER II.	By Rev. A. PLUMMER, M.A.
ST. JOHN: Epistles I., II., and III.	By Rev. W. M. SINCLAIR, M.A.
ST. JUDE	By Rev. A. PLUMMER, M.A.
THE REVELATION	By Rev. Canon BOYD CARPENTER, M.A.

CASSELL & COMPANY, LIMITED, *London; and all Booksellers.*

SELECTIONS FROM

CASSELL & COMPANY'S Publications.

The Early Days of Christianity. By the Ven. Archdeacon FARRAR, D.D., F.R.S. *Ninth Thousand.* Two Vols., demy 8vo, cloth, 24s. (*Can also be had with morocco binding.*)

"The English readers whom he addresses will feel that the charm exerted on them by the 'Life of Christ' and the 'Life of St. Paul' is still kept up in these volumes. They will everywhere find in Canon Farrar a most eloquent and interesting guide, and will rise from the reading of these volumes with a vivid picture of the 'Early Days of Christianity' in their minds."—*Daily News.*

"Presents us with a picture of the 'Church and Society' in the first century of the Christian era, lively, graphic, and interesting. . . . Dr. Farrar has borrowed from contemporary history all the light which it is capable of throwing on the writing of the Apostles."—*Standard.*

The Life and Work of St. Paul. By the Ven. Archdeacon FARRAR, D.D., F.R.S.

LIBRARY EDITION. *Nineteenth Thousand.* Two Volumes, demy 8vo, cloth, 24s.; or bound in morocco, £2 2s.

ILLUSTRATED EDITION. With about 450 Illustrations. £1 1s.; or bound in morocco, £2 2s.

"The real excellences of the book are such as to warrant our recommending its careful study to those who desire to obtain an adequate view of the moral grandeur and complex variety of the Apostle's character, and of the extent and fruitfulness of his labours."—*Guardian.*

The Life of Christ. By the Ven. Archdeacon FARRAR, D.D., F.R.S.

LIBRARY EDITION. *Thirtieth Edition.* Two Vols., demy 8vo, cloth, 24s.; or morocco, £2 2s.

ILLUSTRATED EDITION. With about 300 Original Illustrations. 4to, cloth, gilt edges, 21s.; calf or morocco, £2 2s.

POPULAR EDITION, in One Vol., cloth, 6s.; cloth, gilt edges, 7s. 6d.; Persian morocco, 10s. 6d.; tree calf, 15s.

BIJOU EDITION. Five Vols., cloth, in box, 10s. 6d. the set; or French morocco, 21s.

"Dr. Farrar's qualifications for this great work are in many respects eminent. No thoughtful mind will rise from the perusal of this book without feeling that it reveals a beautiful and harmonious conception. It will serve to raise the mind from mere objections in detail to a comprehensive view of the whole subject."—*Times.*

A Commentary on the Revised Version of the New Testament, for English Readers. By Prebendary HUMPHRY, B.D., Member of the Company of Revisers of the New Testament. 7s. 6d.

Cassell & Company, Limited: Ludgate Hill, London; Paris; and New York.

Selections from Cassell & Company's Publications (continued).

Sermons Preached at Westminster Abbey. By ALFRED BARRY, D.D., D.C.L., Bishop of Sydney, Metropolitan of New South Wales, and Primate of Australia. 360 pages, crown 8vo, cloth, 5s.

Glories of the Man of Sorrows, The. Sermons preached at St. James's, Piccadilly. By the Rev. H. G. BONAVIA HUNT, Warden and Chaplain of Trinity College, London. Cloth, price 2s. 6d.

The Child's Life of Christ. Complete in One handsome Volume, with nearly 300 Original Illustrations. Demy 8vo, cloth gilt, gilt edges, 21s.

The Child's Bible. With 200 ORIGINAL ILLUSTRATIONS. Being a Selection from the Holy Bible, in the Words of the Authorised Version. Cloth, gilt edges, £1 1s. *Cheap Edition*, 7s. 6d.

Cassell's Bible Dictionary. With nearly 600 Illustrations. Crown 4to, 1,159 pages. *Cheap Edition*. Cloth, 7s. 6d.; Half morocco, 10s. 6d.

The Bible Educator. Edited by the Very Rev. Dean PLUMPTRE, D.D. Containing about 400 Illustrations. Complete in Four Vols., cloth, 6s. each.

The Family Bible. With 900 ILLUSTRATIONS. Printed on Fine Toned Paper. Leather, gilt edges, £2 10s.

Cassell's Illustrated Bible. With 900 ILLUSTRATIONS. Royal 4to, 1,476 pages. Persian morocco, gilt edges; or in leather, with corners and clasps.

The Crown Illustrated Bible. With 900 Original Illustrations, executed specially for this Edition. Crown 4to, cloth, 7s. 6d. *Can also be had in Leather Bindings in great variety.*

Bible, The Pew. Cloth, red edges, 5s.; French morocco, red edges, 6s.; French morocco, gilt edges, 7s.; Persian calf, gilt edges, 7s. 6d.; Persian "yapp" gilt edges, 8s.; morocco, gilt edges, 8s. 6d.

Moses and Geology; or, The Harmony of the Bible with Science. By SAMUEL KINNS, Ph.D., &c. With 110 Illustrations. *Seventh Thousand.* Cloth, 10s. 6d.; cloth, gilt edges, 12s. 6d.

The History of Protestantism. By the Rev. J. A. WYLIE, LL.D. Three Vols., with 600 ILLUSTRATIONS. 27s.

Cassell & Company, Limited: Ludgate Hill, London; Paris; and New York.

Roberts's Holy Land. Division I., Jerusalem and Galilee. Division II., The Jordan and Bethlehem. Each containing 42 Tinted Plates. Royal 4to, cloth gilt, 18s. each.

Shortened Church Services and Hymns. Suitable for use at Children's Services. Compiled by the Rev. T. TEIGNMOUTH SHORE, M.A., Chaplain in Ordinary to the Queen. *Enlarged Edition.* Price 1s.

Life of the World to Come, The, and other Subjects. By the Rev. T. TEIGNMOUTH SHORE, M.A. Cloth, 5s.

Keble's Christian Year. Illustrated. Reprinted from the Original Edition. Cloth, 7s. 6d.; gilt edges, 10s. 6d.

The Church at Home. A Series of Short Sermons, with Collect and Scripture for Sundays, Saints' Days, and Special Occasions. By the Right Rev. ROWLEY HILL, D.D., Lord Bishop of Sodor and Man. 5s.

The Quiver. An Illustrated Religious Magazine. Yearly Volumes, 7s. 6d.; also Monthly Parts, 6d.

The Doré Bible. ROYAL 4TO EDITION. Complete in Two Vols., with 220 Illustrations by GUSTAVE DORÉ. Plain morocco, £4 4s.; best morocco, £6 6s.

The History of the English Bible. By the Rev. W. F. MOULTON, M.A., D.D. 2s. 6d.

The Family Prayer Book. *Cheap Edition.* Edited by the Rev. Canon GARBETT, M.A., and the Rev. SAMUEL MARTIN. Extra crown 4to, 398 pp., cloth, gilt edges, 5s.

St. George for England, and other Sermons preached to Children. By the Rev. T. TEIGNMOUTH SHORE, M.A. *Fourth Edition.* Cloth, gilt edges, 5s.

Some Difficulties of Belief. By the Rev. T. TEIGNMOUTH SHORE, M.A., Chaplain in Ordinary to the Queen. *Seventh Edition.* 2s. 6d.

Day-Dawn in Dark Places; or, Wanderings and Work in Bechwanaland, South Africa. By the Rev. JOHN MACKENZIE. Illustrated throughout. Cloth, 3s. 6d.

The Near and Heavenly Horizons. By the Countess DE GASPARIN. 30*th Thousand.* 8vo, stiff paper covers, 1s.; cloth, 2s.

Cassell & Company, Limited: Ludgate Hill, London; Paris; and New York.

Selections from Cassell & Company's Publications (continued).

"Heart Chords." Consisting of Little Books by Eminent Divines, having for their object the stimulating, guiding, and strengthening the Christian Life. Appropriately bound in cloth, red edges, price 1s. each.

My Work for God. By the Right Rev. Bishop COTTERILL.
My Object in Life. By the Ven. Archdeacon FARRAR, D.D.
My Body. By the Rev. Prof. W. G. BLAIKIE, D.D.
My Growth in Divine Life. By the Rev. Prebendary REYNOLDS, M.A.
My Emotional Life. By the Rev. Preb. CHADWICK, D.D.
My Aspirations. By the Rev. GEO. MATHESON, D.D.
My Aids to the Divine Life. By the Very Rev. Dean BOYLE.
My Place in Creation. By the Rev. HUGH MACMILLAN, D.D.
My Bible. By the Rev. Canon BOYD CARPENTER, M.A.
My Soul. By the Rev. P. B. POWER, M.A.
My Hereafter. By the Very Rev. Dean BICKERSTETH.
My Father's House. By the Very Rev. Dean EDWARDS.
My Walk with God. By the Very Rev. Dean MONTGOMERY.
My Sources of Strength. By the Rev. E. E. JENKINS, M.A., Secretary of Wesleyan Missionary Society.
My Father. By the Right Rev. ASHTON OXENDEN, late Bishop of Montreal.

Bunyan's Pilgrim's Progress. With 100 ILLUSTRATIONS by SELOUS and PRIOLO. Cloth, 7s. 6d.

Bunyan's Holy War. With 100 ILLUSTRATIONS by SELOUS and PRIOLO. Cloth, 7s. 6d.

The Young Man in the Battle of Life. By Rev. W. LANDELS, D.D. *Cheap Edition*, 1s.; cloth gilt, 2s.; cloth gilt, gilt edges, 2s. 6d.

Foxe's Book of Martyrs. Edited by the Rev. W. BRAMLEY MOORE, M.A. With Engravings by JOHN GILBERT, MORTEN, EDWARDS, &c. &c. Cloth, 12s.; cloth gilt, 15s.

The Marriage Ring. A Gift-Book for the Newly Married, and for those Contemplating Marriage. By the Rev. WILLIAM LANDELS, D.D. White leatherette, gilt edges, in box, 6s.

The True Glory of Woman. By the Rev. W. LANDELS, D.D. Cloth gilt, gilt edges, 3s. 6d.

The Patriarchs. By the late Rev. W. HANNA, D.D., and the Ven. Archdeacon NORRIS. *Cheap Edition*. Cloth, 2s. 6d.

The Music of the Bible. By JOHN STAINER, M.A., Mus. Doc. *Cheap Edition*. Cloth, 2s. 6d.

History of the Waldenses. By the Rev. J. A. WYLIE, LL.D. With Illustrations. 2s. 6d.

The Voice of Time. By JOHN STROUD. Cloth gilt, 1s.

Shall We Know One Another? By the Right Rev. J. C. RYLE, Lord Bishop of Liverpool. 1s.

☞ COMPLETE CATALOGUES OF CASSELL & COMPANY'S PUBLICATIONS, *containing a List of Several Hundred Volumes, together with a Synopsis of their numerous* ILLUSTRATED SERIAL PUBLICATIONS, *sent post free on application to* CASSELL & COMPANY, LIMITED, *Ludgate Hill, London.*

www.ingramcontent.com/pod-product-compliance
Lightning Source LLC
Chambersburg PA
CBHW022140160426
43197CB00009B/1369